More Praise for *Your Life Isn't for You*

"A brilliantly written and insightful book. Seth's vulnerability and honesty are irresistible—pulling you in and opening your heart to the possibility of a life without walls."

—Michael J. Merchant, President, ANASAZI Foundation

"Weaving his own personal story into Oscar Wilde's great story 'The Selfish Giant,' Seth manages to take profound ideas from moral philosophy and make them accessible to his reader. Those who have found themselves in the dark of this metaphorical winter will find a guide in Seth as he helps show all of us the way out through love."

—Matthew Whoolery, PhD, psychologist and Fulbright Scholar

"Seth's amazing book illustrates a powerful and proven path to happiness and gently reminds us how easily we forget this profound truth: focusing on others brings the deepest joy. Seth's earnestness, humility, and candor capture the essence of what it means to love. I believe it is one of the most important books I have ever read."

—Lindsay Hadley, CEO, Hadley Impact Consulting

"A lot of truth and wisdom in this little book! Seth shares life lessons in a succinct and powerful manner, with a humor that is both entertaining and instructive."

—Sterling C. Tanner, President and Executive Director, Forever Young Foundation

"In a society that seems to be terminally darkened by obsession with one's self, this book shines a quiet light on a profound paradox that is not only a key to finding happiness but a key to truly thriving."

—Nathan Mitchell, MS, LAC, psychotherapist

"Giants being jerks and salmon touching stars and Russia being Russia. These are just a few of the things Seth Adam Smith transforms with his clean, clear prose into a mythology that resounds with Truth—and that's *truth* with a capital *T*."

—Josh Weed, Licensed Marriage and Family Therapist and writer of the blog *The Weed*

"Seth Adam Smith generously shares his thoughts, feelings, and philosophies with unreserved friendliness toward the reader. It's no wonder that Seth continues to gain significant audience interest. His writing is authentic and honest and contains universal truths that initiate positive change in his individual readers."

—Garrett Batty, award-winning writer/director of the inspiring hit film *The Saratov Approach*

"*Your Life Isn't for You* achieves a rare feat: it manages to preach without being preachy and it offers a trove of spiritual lessons that don't require the reader to be 'spiritual.' There's a reason Seth Adam Smith's writing went viral. It's clear and sharp, and maybe most importantly, it asks the big questions about how we can better serve ourselves by serving others."

—Seamus McKiernan, Senior Blog Editor, Special Projects, *The Huffington Post*

"What you will experience as you read this book and any of Seth's writings are a moved heart and a sharper mind. The only thing better than reading the writings of Seth Smith is hanging out with him in person."

—Maurice W. Harker, CMHC, Director, Life Changing Services

"One of the greatest treasures that exist is the offerings given from the heart. Seth has given such a gift. Through the dark labyrinth of depression comes something as soft as the petal of a flower."

—Angela Johnson, sculptor of The Light of the World Garden

"A realistic look at the power of selflessness. Smith's lighthearted language makes the heavy message not just palatable but tasty."

—Meg Johnson, motivational speaker, author, and cofounder of Ms. Wheelchair Utah

"*Your Life Isn't For You* speaks with a simple, practical wisdom born not of academic study, but of richly layered life experience. Seth Adam Smith writes with compassion, authority, and insight, and his style is fresh, humorous, and engaging. His message is relevant to anyone who's ever had a depressing thought—which is all of us."

—Carrie Maxwell Wrigley, LCSW, Morning Light Counseling

Your Life Isn't for You

Other Books by Seth Adam Smith

Marriage Isn't for You

Your Life Isn't for You

A Selfish Person's Guide to Being Selfless

Seth Adam Smith

BK

Berrett–Koehler Publishers, Inc.
San Francisco
a BK Life book

Berrett-Koehler Publishers, Inc.
235 Montgomery Street, Suite 650
San Francisco, CA 94104-2916
Tel: (415) 288-0260 Fax: (415) 362-2512 www.bkconnection.com

Ordering Information
Quantity sales. Special discounts are available on quantity purchases by corporations, associations, and others. For details, contact the "Special Sales Department" at the Berrett-Koehler address above.
Individual sales. Berrett-Koehler publications are available through most bookstores. They can also be ordered directly from Berrett-Koehler: Tel: (800) 929-2929; Fax: (802) 864-7626; www.bkconnection.com
Orders for college textbook/course adoption use. Please contact Berrett-Koehler: Tel: (800) 929-2929; Fax: (802) 864-7626.
Orders by U.S. trade bookstores and wholesalers. Please contact Ingram Publisher Services, Tel: (800) 509-4887; Fax: (800) 838-1149; E-mail: customer.service@ingrampublisherservices.com; or visit www.ingrampublisherservices.com/Ordering for details about electronic ordering.

Printed in the United States of America

Berrett-Koehler books are printed on long-lasting acid-free paper. When it is available, we choose paper that has been manufactured by environmentally responsible processes. These may include using trees grown in sustainable forests, incorporating recycled paper, minimizing chlorine in bleaching, or recycling the energy produced at the paper mill.

Library of Congress Cataloging-in-Publication Data

Smith, Seth Adam.
Your life isn't for you : a selfish person's guide to being selfless /
Seth Adam Smith. — First Edition.
pages cm
Summary: "Following up on his monster blog post "Marriage is Not for You" (30 million views and coverage in broadcast and online media worldwide), Smith shows how the philosophy of living for others he put forward in that post applies to all areas of life"— Provided by publisher.
ISBN 978-1-62656-095-6 (paperback)
1. Selfishness. 2. Benevolence. 3. Kindness. I. Title.
BJ1535.S4S65 2014
170'.44—dc23 2014019293

First Edition

19 18 17 16 15 14 10 9 8 7 6 5 4 3 2 1

Cover design: Ian Koviak/The Book Designers
Author photo: Dmitry Ternovoy
Interior design and composition: Leigh McLellan Design
Copyediting: Elissa Rabellino

••••

Your Life Isn't for You is a book about me learning that my life isn't for me, it's for others.

So, I guess this book is for you?

Contents

Disclaimer

Your life isn't for you.

Really. It's not. Your life isn't for you and my life isn't for me. The truth is that nature didn't design us to find fulfillment in living for ourselves. We can achieve the fullest measure of life only by living it for others.

Sucks, doesn't it?

Well, I think it does. But maybe that's because I am not what you would call a people person. To be perfectly honest, people annoy me. I would much rather work alone in my garden than spend an hour or two socializing. So in a twist of irony, the philosophy I'm about to describe to you—this idea of living your life for others—is one that goes against the flow of my personality. If I were to have it my way, I never would have written a book like this. In fact, I'd probably be living in a cabin in the middle of the Alaskan wilderness with a pack of domesticated wolves trained to keep the humans away.

But I have learned—through sad and brutal experience—the dangers of taking my preference for solitude to extremes. Instead of my introversion being a healthy need for boundaries and personal reflection, it became an obsessive demand for control and isolation. I began to selfishly live my life purely for myself, and it nearly cost me everything. It was only after I nearly succeeded in taking my life, through an attempted suicide, that I stumbled across this life-giving philosophy about selflessness.

Now I need to pause here and define what being selfless means, because it's probably conjuring up images of building orphanages, donating your money and possessions to charity, and performing humanitarian efforts under extreme conditions.

But that's not what being selfless really means—not exactly, anyway. While those things can certainly be selfless actions, they are just that: actions. Actions and behaviors can be mimicked or faked for selfish purposes. A person can travel to another country and do humanitarian work for a photo op or publicity, while others can perform lifesaving services for money, connections, or other ulterior motives.

Honest selflessness is much deeper than our actions—it's a condition of our heart. Being selfless is about opening yourself up to others and learning how to receive life from them and give life back to them. True selflessness is perhaps one of the most paradoxical things in nature: You don't lose yourself for being selfless—you find yourself. You don't lose everything for being selfless—you gain everything. Your life doesn't diminish as you live it for others—it expands.

In short: to give life is to truly live life. This book offers a philosophy of how that can be done.

Introduction

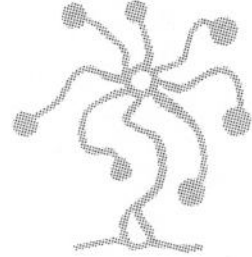

Two million views. I stared at my smartphone in shock. My article "Marriage Isn't for You" was going viral.

It was November 3, 2013. I had been visiting my family in Utah for Halloween and was on a flight back to my home in Florida. My transfer flight had just landed in Baltimore. As soon as the flight attendant gave the OK, I turned on my phone and immediately saw that my blog had received nearly 2.2 million views in thirty-six hours. Every time I refreshed the screen, the stats had gone up not by hundreds but by thousands—tens of thousands.

In three days, the article received a staggering twenty-four million views. It was reprinted in the *Huffington Post* and was prominently featured and discussed on the *Today* show, BuzzFeed.com, *Daily Mail, Cosmopolitan,* MSN Living, Yahoo,

Deseret News, Today.com, KSL News, TheBlaze.com, HuffPost Live, HLN, and numerous radio programs.

On top of all that, Kim, my wife, joined me for national television interviews with *Fox & Friends* and *Good Morning America*.

The article has been translated—by volunteers—into more than twenty languages and has gone viral (one hundred thousand views) in the German, Slovak, Czech, Portuguese, and Spanish languages. As of the spring of 2014, with all the reprints and translations, "Marriage Isn't for You" had well over thirty million hits.

But why? What was it about the message that transcended cultural differences and resonated with millions of people around the world? Why did my article go viral?

Well, first of all, it wasn't really my article that went viral because it wasn't really my message. It was my dad's.

It was counsel given to me in a moment of indecision—at a time when I was debating whether or not I should marry Kim. Was she the right person to marry? Would she make me happy?

My father answered these questions with the advice that has gone viral: "Seth, you're being totally selfish. So I'm going to make this really simple: Marriage isn't for you. You don't marry to make yourself happy, you marry to make someone else happy. . . . It's not about you. Marriage is about the person you married."

His counsel was life changing. It went completely against the grain of my selfish fears. Perhaps that's why his advice resonated with so many people. Because I think we all recognize—

on some level—that selflessly loving others is the right thing to do.

Yes, my dad's advice saved me from selfishness, but it wasn't the first time that he had done so. Five years earlier, my dad had pulled me from a car and dialed 911. When the ambulance arrived at my house, the EMTs immediately began the process of emptying my stomach. I had swallowed a full bottle of sleeping pills and half a bottle of painkillers. I had just tried to take my life.

Before that day, I had been living a life of abject selfishness. I thought only about myself, my wants, my feelings, and my problems. My selfishness was a downward spiral that led to a veritable prison of isolation and despair. Unable to find my way out of the darkness and depression, I decided to end the pain and kill myself.

When I woke up in the hospital the next morning, I was surrounded by my family members. Brokenhearted as they were, and unsure and untrained in how to respond, they nevertheless rallied to support me as best they could.

I had become so self-absorbed that I had walled myself off to everyone and eventually tried to take my life. But standing outside those walls of my selfishness were people willing to give their time, energy, and lives to preserve mine. Although it was incomprehensible to me at the time, my life somehow meant something to other people. My life wasn't for me—it belonged to other people as well. If I was to truly recover from trying to take my life, I needed to learn how to give my life away.

But how? How do selfish people (like me) move from selfishness to selflessness? For one thing, it's not an event—it's a journey. And while I'm certainly not the shining example of selflessness, my experiences have brought me in contact with the lives and literature of those who are. Their examples have been like the Northern Lights in my life—they have lit my path and guided me forward.

So even though I will share many of my own personal experiences, this book really isn't about me. It's about the people, literature, and events that have taught me this life-giving philosophy.

But before I get into that, I feel compelled to address a few things. First, in this book I will talk about serious matters such as depression and suicide. What I share, I share from experience and not from professional training. If you or someone you know is suffering from depression or suicidal thoughts, this book and the principles it espouses are not intended to be used as substitutes for professional medical help. Many of the things I share in this book are things I learned while I was receiving proper medical attention. If you are struggling with depression or suicidal thoughts, I strongly urge you to reach out to trusted friends and seek professional help.

Second, it must be understood that I'm a very selfish person, which is probably why my editors chose the subtitle that they did.[1] But remember, it was not *my* advice but my father's advice that went viral. In like manner, it is not my actions that

---

1. After reviewing this line, my editor, Neal, confirmed it by saying "Guilty!"

are exemplary but the actions of others. It is through them that I have learned these principles, and it is my experiences with them that I will share with you.

Finally, not only am I a very selfish person, but also I'm a very sarcastic person. And although I fully believe in this philosophy that I'm about to share with you, it doesn't change the fact that it sometimes sounds a little too peace-love-hippie-happy, even for me. So, my publisher has graciously agreed to give me space in the footnotes to add my occasional . . . commentary.

All right! I think that's everything. Ready to lose your life?[2] Let's begin!

2. My editors want me to make it clear that I'm not threatening you. It's a play on the title. The first of many. Buckle up.

Your Life Isn't for You

1

The Selfish Giant

In one degree or another we all struggle with selfishness. Since it is so common, why worry about selfishness anyway? Because selfishness is really self-destruction in slow motion.

—NEAL A. MAXWELL, AUTHOR

I was born with a frighteningly large head.

Seriously. It scared the nurse.

Not long after my grand entrance, she measured my head and whispered, "No, that can't be right."

She measured it again. "It's not possible."

She measured it a third time and then looked up at the doctor. "Do you realize that this boy has the biggest head I have ever measured?"[3]

---

3. In the background, my poor mother (who gave birth to me without any sort of painkillers) deliriously shouted, "Tell me about it!"

It was a symbol of things to come. From ill-conceived notions in my six-year-old brain about my ability to create and control a bonfire behind my house to fanciful ideas that made me think I could befriend particularly aggressive wildlife,[4] my big, egotistical head was always getting me into disastrous trouble.

Yes, my giant head was always getting me into trouble. But luckily, my family was always there to bail me out.

I think my father realized that if he didn't do something (beyond the usual punishments), then his son's self-centered ideas could very well lead to self-destruction. My dad needed something that could possibly rewire his child's brain—something that would definitively teach the child: Selfishness, bad. Selflessness, good.

But what? Clearly, his child didn't understand physical punishment, nor did he seem to understand words like "No!" "Stop!" or "You're going to burn the house down!"

No, my dad needed a different, more covert approach. He needed to teach me virtues without my knowledge. That's when it hit him: what better way to teach virtues than to read from *The Book of Virtues*? Surely this eight-hundred-page monstrosity contained the remedy for even the most obstinate of children.

And so, for the one and only time that I can remember, my dad sat down and read a bedtime story to my sister Jaimie and me.

The story was "The Selfish Giant," and it was written by the Irish author Oscar Wilde. Now, I'm a lover of literature. I love

---

4. I tried to feed a bull moose some apples. Incidentally, I once believed that moose were gentle giants. They are not. They are lawless animals.

all kinds of stories, novels, and works of nonfiction. But looking back, I don't think that any other story has had more of an impact on my life.

The story is about a Giant with a large, beautiful garden. While the Giant was away, the local children would gather in his garden and play. "How happy we are here!" they cried to each other.

One day, the Giant came back. "What are you doing here?" said the Giant angrily, and the children ran away. He built a high wall around his garden to keep out any would-be trespassers. In time, the Giant decided to tear down the wall.

As my dad continued to read the story, it soon became apparent that he had never actually read it for himself. I knew this because as he reached the end, he started to get choked up.

Jaimie and I exchanged nervous glances. What was happening to Dad? Seriously. Our dad was the Stonewall Jackson of emotion. He had served in the Marine Corps and worked in the Criminal Investigation Division (CID). He carried out drug busts with a German shepherd named Happy.[5] My dad had seen some crazy stuff and rarely showed his emotion. Getting choked up over a children's story? Something was clearly wrong.

"Uh, Dad?" asked Jaimie. "Is everything OK?"

"I'm fine," my dad replied. He hurriedly finished the story and closed the book. "Good night."

Whatever lesson my dad had tried to teach was tossed aside as we grappled with the fact that our ex-Marine father was

5. The irony of the name was intentional, because working in the CID wasn't like working for Willie Wonka.

probably having an emotional breakdown. We sat in silence, staring at *The Book of Virtues* as though it were the *Book of the Dead*.

It seemed to stare back at us.

"The book broke Dad," Jaimie whispered.

We agreed that the book was evil and resolved to never read from its dark pages. Which is partly why I've carried it with me ever since.[6]

But apart from the very real possibility that the book has dark, magical powers, there is another reason why I've held on to it for all these years. You see, as strange as it was to see my dad get choked up over a children's story, it wasn't the first time I had seen him express emotion. The first time had been a couple of years earlier. Actually, I can give you the exact date.

November 9, 1989.

I was absently playing with my toys when I wandered into my parents' room and found my dad sitting in his chair, positively glued to the TV.

I followed his gaze. What I saw confused me. It was a news report from a foreign country; despite the weather being overcast, cold, and gray, a crowd of people were laughing, smiling, and dancing. The reporter was saying things like "this is truly amazing," "a new beginning," and "a great day."

"What's happening, Dad?" I asked.

"They're tearing it down," he said, his voice heavy with emotion.

I looked back at the screen and saw it: a wall.

---

6. True story. The book is currently on the corner of my writing desk.

The Berlin Wall.

Years later, I would learn the significance of the Berlin Wall. It was built at the height of the Cold War, a forty-year period of icy relations between the Soviet Union and the United States. The Soviets had built the wall to keep East Berlin (occupied by the Soviet Union) separate from West Berlin (occupied by England, France, and the United States). The wall quickly became a hated symbol of the political tensions between the Soviet Union and the West.

After living in Berlin for two years (1966–1968), my dad had become well acquainted with those political tensions. He firmly believed that the United States and Soviet Union would never see eye-to-eye. In his mind, the only way that wall would come down would be through all-out war. So when he saw images of West Berliners helping East Berliners tear down the wall, he almost couldn't believe it.

"The war is over," he whispered.

Ultimately, my dad's inexplicable emotion over these two walls is what prompted me to hold on to the story of "The Selfish Giant." I wanted to know why. Why did a children's story about a giant knocking down a wall mean so much to my dad? Why did a news report about people tearing down a real wall make him shed tears?

The answers to these questions didn't come until almost fifteen years later—when I suddenly and painfully realized that I had been living the story of "The Selfish Giant."

2

Winter within the Wall

To love at all is to be vulnerable. Love anything, and your heart will certainly be wrung and possibly be broken. If you want to make sure of keeping it intact, you must give your heart to no one . . . The only place outside of Heaven where you can be perfectly safe from all the dangers and perturbations of love is Hell.

—C. S. LEWIS, THE FOUR LOVES

I hated being a Mormon missionary.

Hated it.

It was 2005. I was nineteen years old, and I was serving as a missionary in far eastern Russia, near the city of Vladivostok. To say that my father was shocked would be a bit of an understatement. Never in his wildest dreams did he imagine that his own son would one day be living as a missionary in Russia.

Now, some of you might scratch your heads at this contradiction. Wait, didn't Seth tell us that he's an introvert? Doesn't being a missionary demand that you interact with people?

Why yes, yes it does. But despite the image of smiling, singing missionaries in the musical The Book of Mormon, not all of us are as happy-go-lucky about serving a mission.

But the call to serve others is an integral part of my Mormon faith, and I was hopeful that I would somehow (perhaps miraculously) rise to the occasion.

Alas, I didn't exactly soar with the eagles.[7]

In fact, I spent most of my time wandering the streets of Russia with my eyes to the ground and my mouth clamped shut. I woke up as late as I could, spoke with Russians as little as possible, and hurried to bed as soon as I could. I lay there for hours, filled with an intense feeling of dread about what fresh hell the next day would bring.

About halfway through my two-year mission, I felt that I had reached a mental breaking point. In time, I would be diagnosed with chronic depression: a genetic predisposition to feel sad, anxious, worthless, and lonely. Depression runs in my family, and I had unknowingly struggled with the condition for many years. But at the age of nineteen, I didn't know that was what it was. All I knew was that I was hurting, and my mind, in a frantic attempt to find out what was wrong, would dig up hundreds of reasons why I might be sad and worthless. This never-ending stream of thoughts only intensified my feelings of depression.

---

7. In fact, I probably behaved more like an overweight pigeon.

I felt like I was damaged. I thought if people knew who I really was, and if they knew what was going on inside my head, they wouldn't be my friends. So in response to these thoughts and feelings, I did what so many people with depression do: I began to isolate myself from others.

Little did I know that I would soon be entering one of my most severe struggles with depression—one that would last for almost two years.

There's a reason why I'm telling you all this, and that reason came shortly after I met another missionary by the name of Erich. He was a very friendly and humble man from Switzerland, and although he was several inches shorter than me, he had the persona of a gentle giant. Something about him seemed to draw others to him. He would listen to people and they would listen to him. Even those who didn't want to talk to missionaries (and were very vocal about it),[8] if they talked to Erich, not only softened but brightened a little.

I couldn't understand it. How was this quiet, gentle missionary so effective at talking to people? What was it about him that was drawing others to him?

One day, Erich and I were working together in the city of Ussuriysk. On a whim, I asked him what it was that made him such a successful missionary.

Erich looked at me thoughtfully and blinked. "Well . . . I don't know if I'm 'successful,'" he said. "But I do know that the

---

8. Maybe you're one of those vocal people. Don't worry. I don't blame you. I normally hide behind the refrigerator when the Jehovah's Witnesses come to my house. Sorry, guys.

only thing that matters is that you learn to love people. If you learn to love the people you are serving, then everything will just fall into place."

I'd like to say that those words hit me like a ton of bricks—that they changed my life from that moment on—but they didn't. I brushed them off with several sweeps of sarcastic thoughts. Hmph! I thought. OK, yeah, love thy neighbor and all that nonsense.[9] Seriously, though. What does he do? Is there, like, a system? A special way of communicating with people? What books has he been reading? Give me something I can work with!

I've since realized that when I was asking Erich how to be a successful missionary, I was really hoping he would tell me how I could "have it all" but without any of the people.

I was thinking like the Selfish Giant in Oscar Wilde's story. I wanted a beautiful garden (a rich and abundant life) without the annoyance of people trampling through it. It was as though I was asking Erich for tips and tricks on how to improve my garden: How can I have a more abundant harvest? How can I increase the flowers and fruits? And like the Giant, I didn't want people messing up the garden of my life. Excuse me, this is mine. Why are you stomping about? No, no! You're going to ruin everything. Back off! Get out!

But Erich had hinted at the inescapable truth: A garden is beautiful only when it is filled with people; they determine

9. Apparently, some religious guy made a big deal about it. Whatever.

its beauty. Our joy in life is inextricably determined by the degree to which we love and embrace others.[10]

But Erich was asking the impossible. Learn to love these people? Am I not doing enough by simply being here? What more am I expected to give?

As the months dragged on, I continued to build a wall around my heart—quietly pushing people out of my life.

In August, I was transferred to Nakhodka, a small port city tucked away in the most beautiful and peaceful harbor you can imagine. The very name Nakhodka can be translated as "Eureka!" or "Lucky find."

But despite the city's name and natural serenity, I found no peace and no rest there. A storm was raging in my heart. Because of the cultural differences[11] and the overwhelming

---

10. In a satirical article, "How to Be Unhappy," for ForwardWalking.com, my friend Matthew Whoolery, a professor of psychology, said, "Many religious teachers—from Buddha to Jesus—have taught you to forget yourself. The key to unhappiness is to pretend that they simply didn't mean any of it. You must reinterpret Buddhist teachings to mean that you must seek only for your own enlightenment. Then do the wonderful word-dance to reinterpret the Christian teaching of 'love thy neighbor as thyself' to actually mean 'love yourself before you can love your neighbor.' This will help immensely in your search for unhappiness."
11. Seriously. Russians are like coconuts and Americans are like peaches. Russians are often very tough on the outside but softhearted and sweet on the inside. In contrast, some Americans may act very soft and sweet on the outside but can harbor a hardened inside. Like me when I was struggling in Russia.

resistance from Russians to even listen to us, I had taken offense toward them. My hostility only increased their resistance toward me.

In October, I was overcome by a terrible fever. Its intensity, pain, and duration were unlike anything I had ever experienced. I was delirious. I was in the most excruciating pain, immobile, and perpetually drenched in sweat. The Russians who knew about my condition did everything in their power to help me. During a three-week period, they visited me often and recommended a host of Russian doctors, medicines, and remedies.[12]

You would think that after weeks of enduring such pain, I would eagerly accept help from any source. But I didn't. In fact, I flat-out rejected any help that came from Russians. Part of that stemmed from sheer arrogance: how could Russian medicines be better than American medicines?

But there was another, more cynical reason why I rejected Russian aid. You see, I wanted irrefutable justification for my bitterness. I wanted to have some legitimate reasons to push Russians out of my life and prove that I was right and they were wrong. Instead of wanting to be healthy, I wanted to be right.

Looking back on it now, I often wonder if that sickness was a manifestation of a much deeper sickness in my heart.

---

12. On a very serious note, while reviewing this manuscript, I painfully remembered one Russian woman who brought me a store-bought cake, hoping that it would help cheer me up. This was a hard thing to remember because store-bought cakes were very expensive, and the woman who brought it to me was not only extremely poor but also mentally challenged. It hurts my heart to think about it.

As I started to get better physically, I made the decision to leave Russia and return to the States. I was done. I obviously wasn't designed to love people, and I was only causing problems there. My inability to "love people" had frustrated me for the last time. Why keep it up? Why try anymore?

In November 2005, after lying to myself and others, I turned my back on Russia and boarded a plane for the States.

But there was a hollowness to my homecoming. Though I stood in the house in which I had grown up, something inside of me was lost. In coming home early, I was unknowingly following in the footsteps of the Selfish Giant. After a prolonged absence, the Giant "determined to return to his own [home]." But there was a bitterness to his homecoming—a winter in his return.

Once the Giant had finished building his wall, it underwent a bitter transformation. While the surrounding townsfolk enjoyed the blossoms and birds of spring, it was as if the season had intentionally neglected the garden of the Giant. "The birds did not care to sing in it as there were no children, and the trees forgot to blossom."

Sitting by his window and looking out at his cold, white garden, the Selfish Giant couldn't understand why the spring was so late in coming. And although he hoped for a change in weather, "the Spring never came, nor the Summer. The Autumn gave golden fruit to every garden, but to the Giant's garden she gave none."

In the weeks and months that followed my return from Russia, I spent most days lying in bed, trying to sleep my life away. I was bruised by my decision to emotionally wall off my heart and distance myself from other people. My world began to wither and my relationships started to rot.

It didn't seem logical to me. I thought my decision to come home was the best thing for me and for others. Why would anyone want to deal with my depression, anyway? Who could love someone like me? Since I had so little to give other people, why not protect what little life I had? Wouldn't sharing my life mean that I lost it? I made my decision to protect others as much as myself, so why was I feeling so depressed?

All around me, people lived and laughed as though it was spring and summer. But I would look out the window of my life, and, like the Selfish Giant, I could only see a dark and wintry world.

This internal winter became so oppressive that I lost all sense of sentiment. Instead, all I felt was just all-consuming emptiness. Overcome by the need to fill this void, I sought any means of escape or relief, and I quickly became addicted to painkillers.

My addiction only accelerated my desire to serve myself, driving me further and further into isolation, secrecy, and self-centeredness.

In his short story, Oscar Wilde masterfully illustrates the pain and isolation of depression through the use of four characters that personify different elements: Snow, Frost, the North Wind, and Hail.

"Spring has forgotten this garden," they cry, "so we will live here all year round." They then take turns gleefully beating down the garden and home of the Selfish Giant.

In a similar way, I felt like all of my life was being beaten out of me—as though all the color in my life was fading away. Entirely focused on the theater of my own wintry world, I grew numb to the needs of others and started to crumble against the onslaught of depression.

Then one day, after years of carefully constricting my own world into a sphere of suffocating selfishness, I decided that I could no longer endure the winter. It was at this point that I made the decision to commit suicide.

I went to work that day; gave a dull nod to Ariel, my sister-in-law and supervisor; clocked in for about an hour; and then clocked out. I drove home, parked the car in the garage, and scribbled goodbye letters in my journal as I took half a bottle of painkillers and a full bottle of sleeping pills.

Once I had finished, I went into the garage and climbed into the car, fully believing that I would never open my eyes again. At the same time, my dad was at work when he was overcome with a feeling of intense dread. He called everyone in the family but couldn't get hold of me. Unable to shake the ominous feeling, my dad left his office and came to the house.

Finding the empty bottles on the counter, he went from room to room, frantically searching bathrooms, closets, and even under beds.

When he got to the garage, it was so dark that he could barely see me reclined in the driver's seat of the car. As soon as he recognized me, he rushed to the car, opened the door, and started to pound my chest.

Lost in a drug-induced haze, I could vaguely feel several dull thuds on my chest and lazily opened my eyes. I saw the outline of my dad and distantly heard him shouting my name. He pulled me out of the car. I staggered forward and collapsed. He lifted me up and shook me to prevent me from going to sleep.

At one point, I remember being on my bed and hearing my dad on the phone with my mother: "Lyn, come quick! Seth's hurt! I think he tried to take his life!" Then he called 911.

The next thing I remember was being on the couch in the living room, surrounded by three paramedics. Between their movements I saw my three-year-old niece, Kelty, eyes wide, holding a juice box—my mother had brought her to the house. Amid the noise and clatter I heard my mother sob, "Seth, what have you done?!"

I have a distant memory of being given something to clean the drugs out of my system as I was rushed to the hospital. I saw my brother Sean in the ER with me. Tears were rolling down his cheeks.

Looking back on it now, I shudder to think how close I came to ending my life. I would have succeeded had my father not found me.

You see, despite my efforts to make my life "my own," there were people who valued my life as though it were their own. They had already learned that their lives were not just for them and had wrapped their hearts around mine, whether or not I chose to accept it.

I remember waking up in the hospital that night and realizing that I had failed to commit suicide. Not only was the weight of winter still omnipresent, but I felt that my failure to commit suicide had now brought my family into my circle of pain. Overcome by a fresh wave of grief and despair, I buried my face in my hands and wept without restraint.

As I awoke in the hospital the next morning, I had no idea that the real awakening was about to begin. The doctors and hospital equipment may have preserved my life, but my family was about to give me one that was far more abundant.

3

A Melted Heart

The notion that our lives are like the eternal cycle of the seasons does not deny the struggle or the joy, the loss or the gain, the darkness or the light, but encourages us to embrace it all—and to find in all of it opportunities for growth.

—PARKER PALMER, *LET YOUR LIFE SPEAK*

One morning, the Selfish Giant woke up to music so sweet that "he thought it must be the King's musicians passing by." In reality, it was the singing of a little bird in his garden—a sound that signified the coming of spring, and one he had not heard for many years. He ran to his window and "saw a most wonderful sight."

The children had discovered a hole in the wall and had crawled back into the garden. And, as if by magic, anything that the children touched burst into life. "The birds were flying about and twittering with delight, and the flowers were looking up through the green grass and laughing."

Seeing this, the Giant's heart melted and he cried out, "How selfish I have been!" Although the Giant had built what he had imagined to be an impenetrable wall, the children had found a way to come back. The stony wall around his heart was eventually penetrated by the love and humanity of others.

In the weeks and months that followed my suicide attempt, I watched in wonder as my tenderhearted family rallied around me. They had offered me love before, but I had rejected it as I callously hid behind my wall.

But as weak and vulnerable as I was, my family had caught a glimpse of my wintry soul. They mounted an urgent rescue mission to find any opening in my defenses so they could offer the surest and purest form of life support: love.

Looking back on it all, I've sometimes wondered about my parents' reaction to the situation—what my mother must have been feeling when she sobbed, "Seth, what have you done?!" My mom and dad certainly knew that I was in pain and had expressed their concern for me on multiple occasions, but they hadn't known the extent of my struggles because I had been hiding them from everyone. As my mother later described, my suicide attempt "took the air out of [her] chest."

What would my reaction have been? What would I have done if someone I loved tried to take his life? How would I help him? What would my solution be?

Shortly after I started writing this book, I asked my mom what she had been feeling at the time. I asked her what she, as a parent, felt she needed to do.

"When I saw you on the couch," she began, "with all of the paramedics around, I felt like all of the air had been taken out of my chest. I just felt so helpless and powerless. We didn't know that you would be OK until the doctors told us. But even after they told us you were going to make it, I was still worried. The drugs in your body caused you to go in and out, and every time you came back, you would cry and tell us that you didn't want to be here . . . that you didn't want to live.

"I didn't know what to do. I've never struggled like that before. I've never wanted to end my life. I didn't know how to help my own son."

At this point, she got teary. "But then I remembered something that my mother had told me many years ago when I was struggling with a different situation. She said, 'Lyn, just love. You can't know everything, but you can love. So just love.'"

So that's what she did.

And standing where I am today, I can say that love is what saved my life. Love is what freed me from the cell of my selfishness; love is what melted my heart. Just love. That's it. When we are locked in the prison of our heart, no key, no tool, no resource, is more liberating than love.

After my suicide attempt, I frequently visited both a counselor and a psychologist, and I was given a prescription drug to help treat my depression. Those things were important steps to my recovery. But I honestly can't credit them with saving my life. They were helpful and needful, to be sure. But they were like the lifelines that someone uses to save another person from drowning. Lifelines aren't the things that save lives. Ultimately, it's the people who throw us the lifelines that are responsible for saving our lives.

Like small seeds, small deeds can make a big difference. For example, coming home from the hospital, Sean helped me from the car and then into the house. When I told him that he didn't have to stay, he was quiet for a while before saying, "Seth, I almost lost my little brother yesterday. I'm not going anywhere for a while."[13]

My mother, at age fifty-eight, spent several nights sleeping on the floor next to me, just to make sure I'd have someone to talk to. Although I remained stoic and selfish, these tender experiences began to thaw my wintry heart.[14]

But for all my talk about love and family support, I realize that I've been very lucky. Not all people have a supportive family. In fact, some of you might be dealing with problems that are the direct result of poor family relationships. You may feel alone, depressed, and bruised because of your family.

To those who are struggling with family relationships, I want you to know that you're not alone. Most, if not all, of us are struggling—on some level—with family relationships. I was

---

13. Sean wants me to add the fact that he followed up with "Don't do anything stupid like that ever again, butt munch."

14. About a month later, Sean invited me over to his house, where we watched *Better Off Dead*, a quirky comedy about a high school student who unsuccessfully tries to kill himself multiple times. About halfway through the movie, Sean turned to me and said, "Uh, I'm not sure if you should be watching this." I laughed. Quite the contrary. The humor was *exactly* what I needed.

the recipient of the love and support of my family, but on the flip side, they were receiving pain and rejection from me.

But family isn't just about blood. Some of our closest friends can be like family. Indeed, after all that my family had done to bring life back to me, it was the words from a friend that made me fully understand what I had been doing to myself.

While my family was working with me, my best friend, Jeff, was living halfway across the world in Bangkok, Thailand. Jeff and I had been buddies ever since middle school. During that time, we ditched a lot of classes, ate a lot of pizza, and got into more trouble than our mothers will ever know about.[15] Ever.[16]

But despite our apparent immaturity, his response to my troubles was like a lifeline—a light in the wilderness.[17] I printed it out and read it almost every day for a year. Here is part of his e-mail:

> I don't know what to say, my friend. I want to help so bad. I want to be there so bad. I want to sneak out and pick you up to go to Wendy's and laugh about old times and plan crazy stupid things for the future. Especially the Wendy's part, rice just isn't the same. . . . We had such good times, my friend. I've told you how grateful I am for that and I'll tell you again. You've been a light in my life. Don't ever forget what a true giant you really are.

---

15. Mom, of course I'm kidding.

16. Seriously.

17. See chapter 9.

Sometimes, the best advice is like the detonator of a most beautiful destruction. Jeff's last sentence rippled through me like a revelatory shockwave.

His statement that I was "a true giant" instantly reminded me of the Selfish Giant. The remembrance illuminated the frozen wasteland of my life, exposing the hard truth: I had become just like the Selfish Giant.

I thought about all the problems that had brought me to that point, and then I thought about Sean, my mother sobbing, and the frantic yelling of my dad as he desperately tried to revive me.

For the first time since coming home from Russia, I realized just how much I had been hurting other people. Like the Giant in the story, I had selfishly tried to hoard the life that was "mine." Instead of giving my life, I had gone so far as to try to take my life completely.

In so doing, I had pushed out the people who loved me the most—innocent and kindhearted people who wanted nothing more than to love me and have me be a part of their lives.

And just as in Oscar Wilde's story, loving people had managed to find their way back into the garden of my heart. Perhaps they had spent months on the other side, patiently chipping away at parts of my wall.

After I woke up in the hospital, I became the recipient of an outpouring of love from multiple sources: parents, siblings, friends, and neighbors. The contrast of life was so unbelievably different than what I had been experiencing. It was like believing that the darkness of your winter would never end and then feeling the sunshine of spring.

In that light, I suddenly saw the wall around my heart for what it was. Like the Giant, I could finally realize, "How selfish I have been!"

But in the midst of that awful clarity there was great reason to hope. For if my life was truly comparable to the isolation of the Giant, it also meant that my life was equally comparable to his eventual liberation.

In that moment, I became aware of a terrible, beautiful truth: I had the power to choose. I could choose the level of life and light that I was willing to receive. I know this because I had already done it. I had chosen to follow in the footsteps of the Giant. I had chosen to push people out of my life. I had chosen to build a wall around my heart. And if I had decided to build the wall around my heart, then I could also decide to tear it down. The choice was mine. Would I continue to take my life for myself, or would I give it away to others? And if I chose to give it away, where would I begin?

The story of the Selfish Giant pointed the way . . .

4

Look Out the Window

How much larger your life would be if your self could become smaller in it. . . . You would break out of this tiny and tawdry theatre in which your own little plot is always being played, and you would find yourself under a freer sky.

—G. K. CHESTERTON, *ORTHODOXY*

Looking out the window of his home, the Giant saw a little boy who was unable to climb a tree and join his friends. The little boy's eyes were full of tears. At the sight of this, "the Giant's heart melted" and he "crept downstairs and opened the front door quite softly and went out into his garden."

The Giant was able to abandon his solitary confinement because he had seen the suffering of another. He looked out the window of his lonely world and saw a world beyond himself.

The first step toward liberation is as easy as looking out the window of your own life. See how others might be suffering, and then open the door to go out and help them. My sister Shannon gave me a key that helped me open my door—actually, she gave me a keychain.

Shannon is the oldest in our family and was born with a moderate form of cerebral palsy. This condition has caused her to struggle with a severe learning disability and has made it difficult for her to walk straight. Shannon is as gentle and innocent as a child; she's one of the most charitable and loving people I've ever known.

Not long ago, she sent me this tender e-mail:

> I have a learning disability. I went through special ed. Through elementary, Jr. high and high school. I had to work really hard. I am thankful for my family for their love and support they gave me. I graduated from high school with honors. I teach Headstart as a part time Teacher Assistant working with children ages 3–5. I babysit my nieces and nephews. I play the piano by ear. I love to write short stories. You can do anything if you put your mind to it. We all have disabilities in some areas. Some people are able to hide their disability or handicap better than others. I feel everyone is special.

After I tried to take my life, I don't know if Shannon fully understood what had just happened or what she could do to help. But when I came back from the hospital and hobbled into the house, I found a gift from her on my pillow. It was a silver heart-shaped keychain with the word *Moscow* inscribed on it. Taped to the keychain was a note that read, "I hope you get better soon."

I don't know if there's a way for me to convey the value of that little gift. Just as small keys open big doors, sometimes small and seemingly simple things can be catalysts for tremendous change. The keychain reminded me of my own power—of the key that I held in my own hand. That key was my ability to choose to open the door of my solitary confinement and step out into the world.

Not long after I came home from the hospital, I found out that Shannon and her boyfriend had broken up. He wanted to get more serious, but she simply wasn't ready for that kind of commitment. Their relationship had been much more platonic than other dating relationships, but they had spent a lot of time together and had a lot of fun. In many ways, her boyfriend was one of her best friends.

About a week into my recovery, I remember walking past Shannon's room and seeing her with my sister Stephanie. Stephanie is the second oldest in our family, but in many ways it feels like she's the oldest. She went to college, got married, had three daughters, and has a full-time career. While Shannon has always believed that those things would happen for her, her cerebral palsy has created some unique challenges and obstacles. For years, she has watched her younger siblings get married and start families of their own. Breaking up with her boyfriend—who was also her very close friend—was probably much harder for her than I could possibly imagine.

Looking into her room that day, I saw something I would never forget: Shannon was sitting on a small chair while Stephanie stood behind her, brushing her hair. Tears were silently streaming down Shannon's face.

In that moment, I suddenly realized that I wasn't the only person who was suffering. There was a whole world of suffering outside the walls of my own heart. In fact, there was another person who was suffering within the walls of my own home. As I thought about this, I remembered the keychain that Shannon had given me. Even though she was grappling with her own pain, she nevertheless had looked beyond herself to help me.

That's one of the most interesting things about selfishness: When we're constantly thinking about ourselves, our world shrinks and our pain becomes suffocating. But when we think about others, our world expands and our own pain becomes less intense—because it's no longer our primary focus.

The idea of suffocating selfishness was perfectly illustrated in Charles Dickens's *A Christmas Carol*. In the pivotal meeting between Scrooge and the ghost of Jacob Marley, Jacob—now a chained and tortured soul—laments the times when he "walk[ed] through crowds of fellow-beings with [his] eyes turned down." In life, his eyes had been narrowly focused on the world of his financial business. But in death he learned about what should have been his business: "Mankind was my business. The common welfare was my business; charity, mercy, forbearance, and benevolence, were all my business. The dealings of my trade were but a drop of water in the comprehensive ocean of my business."

After the ghost of Jacob Marley departs, Scrooge looks out the window and sees a host of chained and wretched phantoms. "The misery with them all was, clearly, that they sought to interfere, for good, in human matters, and had lost the power for ever."

The rest of the story follows Scrooge as he discovers a world outside of himself—a world in which he has the responsibility to alleviate the suffering of others. As with Ebenezer Scrooge, our hope for happiness in life is tethered to our ability to let go of ourselves and love other people.

In Dostoyevsky's novel *Crime and Punishment,* the main character, Raskolnikov, adopts a selfish philosophy that great men are above certain moral restrictions and obligations. Believing himself to be one of these men, Raskolnikov murders two women and steals a handful of items. He hides all evidence of his crimes and then tries to wipe the blood from his conscience—but he soon discovers that he cannot. His philosophy of selfishness cannot free him from the stain of his crimes. He is overcome with an obsessive, feverish guilt.

Not long after the murders, Raskolnikov meets Sonia, a self-sacrificing woman compelled into prostitution to save her impoverished family. Judging her to be a "sinner" like him, Raskolnikov is drawn to her. After learning about her struggles and pain, Raskolnikov begins to see a world beyond himself and eventually confesses his crimes to Sonia. Her reaction is one of the most sublime moments in all of literature:

> "What have you done—what have you done to yourself!" she said in despair, and, jumping up, she flung herself on his neck, threw her arms round him, and held him tight.
>
> Raskolnikov drew back and looked at her with a mournful smile. "You are a strange girl, Sonia—you kiss me and hug me when I tell you about that. . . . You don't think what you are doing."

> "There is no one—no one in the whole world now so unhappy as you!" she cried in a frenzy, not hearing what he said, and she suddenly broke into violent hysterical weeping.
>
> A feeling long unfamiliar to him flooded his heart and softened it at once. He did not struggle against it. Two tears started into his eyes and hung on his eyelashes.

Notice the irony: Raskolnikov's selfish belief in himself had led to the deaths of two people and was slowly killing him. In marvelous contrast, Sonia's selfless response to Raskolnikov essentially brought him "back from the dead," prompting him to eventually confess to the authorities and giving him hope for the future.

Just as the Selfish Giant looked outside his window and saw the promise of spring, Scrooge and Raskolnikov found hope and renewal as they looked outside of the "windows" of their own lives. When we truly look beyond ourselves, not only will we find a world filled with suffering, but also we will find hope. Because the suffering we see gives us the opportunity to reach beyond ourselves and lift another—for in lifting another person, we also lift ourselves.

5

Lift Another

Within every child is a seed of greatness.

—EZEKIEL SANCHEZ,
COFOUNDER OF THE ANASAZI FOUNDATION

After the Giant opened the door to his solitary confinement, he went to the little boy who could not climb the tree. The Giant "stole up behind him and took him gently in his hand, and put him up into the tree."

I think it's significant that the Giant was able to lift the boy in his hand. In a literal way, the Giant lifted another person—but in reaching out and helping someone else, he symbolically lifted himself in the process.

A story is told of a wise man who could interpret the messages of the wind and hear the thoughts of men. He traveled from kingdom to kingdom, dazzling the villagers with his knowledge and freely sharing his knowledge with the people.

One day, the traveler came to the kingdom of a very prideful king. Jealous of the traveler's fame, the king ordered his guards to arrest the traveler and bring him to his court so that the king could question him in front of all the people.

"Tell me, traveler," began the king, "is it true that you read the messages of the wind?"

"Yes, I can," answered the traveler.

The king snorted. He did not believe that anyone could do such a thing. "And is it true that you can read the thoughts of men?"

"Yes, I can."

"Well then," said the king with a smile. "Behind my back I hold a bird. Tell me—since you are so powerful—is the bird dead or alive?"

The traveler grew quiet and sorrowful, for it was a trap. Reading the king's thoughts, he knew that wicked ruler held a live bird in his hands. If the traveler said that the bird was alive, the king would strangle the bird and show its dead body to the crowd. If the traveler said that the bird was dead, the king would release the bird unharmed.

And so the traveler said the only thing he could say. "The answer is in your hands."

I think that last line is what makes the story so powerful. The answer is in your hands. In like manner, the solutions to many of our problems can be found in our hands—in lifting other people. The complication comes from not knowing exactly how to lift. When is the best time to do something? Who are the most important people to help? What is the most important thing to do?

Leo Tolstoy, the famous Russian novelist and social reformer, asked those very same questions. These were his answers:

> There is only one time that is important—Now! It is the most important time because it is the only time when we have any power. The most necessary man is he with whom you are, for no man knows whether he will ever have dealings with any one else: and the most important affair is, to do him good, because for that purpose alone was man sent into this life! ("Three Questions," in *What Men Live By and Other Tales*)

In other words, worry less about the things outside of your immediate realm of influence. The most important time is now, and the most important person in that moment is the person whom you're with, and the most important thing you can do in that moment is to do that person good. It is as simple as the advice given to me by Erich: "The only thing that matters is that you learn to love people. If you learn to love the people you are serving, then everything will just fall into place."

Often, we're tempted to think that we have little to offer the world. We think that we couldn't possibly help this person or that person because we don't understand their condition or we don't have enough training, influence, resources, or money. The truth is, our ability to love is the very thing that can help lift people out of the darkest corners of their heart. My family wasn't trained in suicide prevention and response, but their small acts of service have had a profound effect on me.[18]

---

18. For crying out loud, I've written about them in this book!

Like seeds, small deeds of light can make a huge tree of life. I discovered this truth in the fall of 2007, when I was working at the ANASAZI Foundation, a wilderness therapy program for at-risk youth.

This program is based in the desert of northeastern Arizona—a far cry from the Alaskan and Russian climates to which I had grown accustomed. In the wilderness, we hiked with and helped teenagers struggling with addiction to drugs or working through depression, eating disorders, anger, or a host of other issues.

Reinforced with trained medical and clinical staff, the program offers a six-week course in nature: primitive skills, organic foods, hiking through canyons, and sleeping under the stars. The time spent in the wilderness allows the youth an opportunity to detox from any drug abuse, and it also allows them the time to quietly consider their own lives.

I had come to work at the program to strengthen my own life. My slow recovery from my suicide attempt was giving me a new sense of purpose: I wanted to try to open up and help others. But after years of living such a shallow life, I frankly didn't know if I had anything to offer.

A few months into the job, I met a young participant whom I'll call Megan. Truth be told, when I first saw Megan, I hoped that I wouldn't be asked to work with her. Even though she was only sixteen years old, Megan looked like a fighter who had gone through hell. Her eyes were heavy-lidded and angry. Everything about her hardened exterior gave me the impression of a spiny saguaro cactus—constantly prepared to defend herself.

As fate would have it, Andrew, our field director, asked me and a few other employees to walk with her for a week. As I was leaving the office to report to the trail, he pulled me aside and encouraged me with these words: "Seth, remember what we always teach: within every child is a seed of greatness. The barriers and fortifications they've placed around that potential may seem intimidating, but the walls without are nothing compared to the potential within."

His words reminded me of the continued efforts of my friends and family to look for the best within me. I resolved to spend the rest of my week with Megan searching for and encouraging all of the good things about her.

At first, it was challenging. Megan was extremely resistant to the program, and we didn't have a lot in common. She had a prickly personality and would often lash out and say derogatory things. But I had determined that this was not about how hard it was for me—it was about how hard things must be for Megan. Lots of people hadn't given up on me for years. Why should I give up on Megan after just a few days?

As I persisted, a most remarkable thing began to happen. The more I got to know Megan and learn about her life, the more I came to respect, admire, and love this girl who had been through so much. I started to understand why she felt that she had to put up defenses. The more I listened to her and tried to understand, the more she seemed to feel that she could lower her defenses.

Toward the end of the week, I sat down with Megan to share with her a list I had made. It was a list of her "seeds of greatness," a compilation of all the great things I had seen within her throughout the week.

It was not a small list.

When I had finished reading the list, I looked up at her and noticed that tears were welling up in her eyes. I was shocked. I hadn't expected that tough girl to react in that way.

"Seth," she whispered, "no one has ever told me anything like that before."

A few weeks later, I met up with Megan as she was finishing the program. Her face was smeared with the dirt and grime of hiking through the wilderness, but she shone like the sun. Her eyes, once heavy-lidded and filled with anger, now glowed with life and light. Megan saw and believed in her seeds of greatness.

I once compared Megan to the saguaro, the prickly, treelike cactus that grows in the Arizona desert. The interesting thing about the saguaro is that for all its defenses, it contains far more life than we might think. For example, on the rare occasions when it rains in the desert, the saguaro visibly expands as it soaks up as much water as it can.

But the saguaro holds another form of secret life. Every June, ripening at the very summit of the saguaro cactus are its hard-to-reach and well-guarded fruits. These fruits not only are incredibly delicious and valuable but also contain overwhelming abundance; each saguaro fruit contains an estimated two thousand seeds.

Since leaving ANASAZI, Megan has gone on to do astonishing things. I hear from her every now and then. She tells me about the travels she's had, the things she's done, the service she's rendered, and the family and friends that she loves.

To hear her talk about the life she is living enriches and fulfills my own life. I was a part of her journey—I walked with her. Within every person is a seed of greatness.

I once heard someone compare our lives to the wheel of a wagon. He said that when we are at the top of the wheel, we should reach down and lift those who are below us. Then, when they reach the top, they will reach out and lift us. This is the only way in which we can truly move forward in life—by reaching out and lifting another.

Just like the Giant or the king, we can find the answers to our lives "in our hands"—in the form of small acts of service that we perform for others. Reach out and lift someone else. See and acknowledge his or her seeds of greatness, for as we lift and inspire other people, we also lift ourselves.

6

Knock Down the Wall

One can choose to go back toward
safety or forward toward growth.
Growth must be chosen again and again;
fear must be overcome again and again.

—ABRAHAM MASLOW, PSYCHOLOGIST

After the Giant had shown the children that he was no longer a selfish Giant, he turned to them and declared, "It is your garden now, little children." He then took his great ax and knocked down the wall.

Each of us has built walls of one form or another. They may be fiercely defensive walls built out of anger and hatred, or they may simply be precautionary walls built out of fear and pain.

Some walls may be justifiable defenses, built to keep you from hurting yourself or being hurt by another. But often, these walls keep out more life than originally intended.

I was made aware of this fact when I was contacted by a Russian girl named Galena, a native of Nakhodka whom I had known while living there.

Galena had moved to the United States to study English and pursue her education. Perpetually peaceful, warm, and serene, Galena is like a living embodiment of the harbor in which she was raised. Friendly as she was, Galena contacted me a number of times, wanting to know how I was doing and maybe hang out. Still embittered by my past experiences, I did my best to wall Galena out of my life. I just didn't want anything to do with Russia.

In the fall of 2007, I received an e-mail from Galena. In it, she said this: "Seth, I pray that you are healthy. Is everything OK with you? If you need any help or someone to talk to, you can always ask me, the door is always open for you. I just want to be your friend."

Imagine how perfectly rotten I felt after reading that. Here I was, earnestly laboring to reinforce a wall that would keep Russians out of my life. And yet, on the other side of that wall stood a Russian girl who promised to always leave the door of friendship open to me.

Galena's words prompted the next stage in my desire to change: I decided to "tear down my wall" (face my fear) by returning to Russia. Over the course of two years, that country had evolved into the embodiment of everything I had feared.

But I was tired of living in fear. I was tired of building walls and hiding behind them.

And so, after doing a bit of research, I found an English teaching program that took me to Moscow, the very heart of Russia (go big or go home, right?). It seemed like a great deal. The only problem with the program was that it required me to live with a Russian host family.

Although my "stranger-danger" alarms were ringing like the Hunchback of Notre Dame on a Monster[19] energy drink, I heard something quite different in a quiet corner of my heart. It was a memory—the gentle voice of Erich: "I do know that the only thing that matters is that you learn to love people. If you learn to love the people you are serving, then everything will just fall into place."

And so, in January 2008—in the middle of a brutal Russian winter—I boarded a plane to Moscow. After a full day of traveling, I met my Russian host family on a street outside of their apartment. The father, Dmitry, was a tall, skinny man with long, wiry dark hair that made him look more like a giant scarecrow than a stereotypical Russian bear.

He grinned and extended his hand. "Welcome to our home," he said in English with a thick Russian accent. The introvert in me wasn't too keen on physical contact, but I forced myself to reach out my hand and shake his.

That small gesture opened the way to a barrier-breaking friendship.

---

19. No pun intended, Quasimodo.

It all started when Dmitry let slip that he was a fan of the *Indiana Jones* movies.

"Seth," he said, "do you want to watch *Indiana Jones* with me and Pasha?"

I was shocked. "*Indiana Jones*?" I repeated. "You like *Indiana Jones*?"

Dmitry looked at me as if I were stupid personified. "They are my favorite movies," he said.

"They're my favorite movies," I said, blown away by the fact that a Russian could like *Indiana Jones*. "They're coming out with a new one in May."

I vividly remember what happened next: Dmitry looked up at me, dropped the papers he was holding, and swore in Russian. "Are you serious?" he said. The tall Russian scarecrow looked as giddy as a little kid.

I grinned and nodded.

"We must see this movie," Dmitry said with fixed determination. "The day it comes out—we must see this movie."

Though the thought of seeing the new *Indiana Jones* movie on opening night in Moscow was thrilling, I was a little nervous.

"Um, Dmitry?" I hedged. "I don't know if we should go see it together."

Dmitry looked affronted. "Why?"

"Well, because the villains are Soviets," I admitted.

Dmitry laughed and waved his hand. "Oh, don't worry. I was a Soviet. I don't like Soviets either. Go, Indy!"

I joined in the laughter, and we sat down and watched *Indiana Jones and the Last Crusade* in Russian.[20]

Later that year, on March 2, Russia held its national elections. The occasion gave me the opportunity to talk to my host dad about a topic I had previously avoided: communism and politics in Russia.

Dmitry had been a child when the Soviet Union dissolved, allowing its numerous republics to govern themselves independently. The Russian Federation itself underwent a dramatic governmental change, transitioning from a communist system to a federal semipresidential constitutional republic. Political power began to shift from a highly centralized system—where all the power is with the politicians—to a decentralized system—where the people would hold the power.

"And that was something that we could not understand," Dmitry said, lowering his cup of tea. "For the first time in our history, the leader of our country was walking among the people.

"For as long as I could remember," he continued, "our leaders would never talk with us. They would only talk to us. And they would tell us that the West was our enemy and we must always be ready to go to war with them. Few of us knew anyone from the West, and few of us had known anything

20. I should mention that we went to *Indiana Jones and the Kingdom of the Crystal Skull* on opening day. We didn't like it. After the movie, Dmitry turned to me and said, "So I guess America finally sent a bomb to Russia!"

outside of our own country. But when Gorbachev became president, everything started to change. Not only would he talk with us, but he would walk among us. He said that he wanted to be more open with the West and with the world.

"When our country opened up to the rest of the world, we started to understand something: People in the world weren't as different from us as we had been told. The West was no longer an enemy, but more like long-lost family."

My host dad was thoughtful for a moment before adding, "This is one of the reasons why we chose to have an American stay with our family—so we could discover how similar we are."

Sitting in that kitchen in Moscow, munching on wafers and sipping tea with Dmitry, I again remembered Erich's words: "I do know that the only thing that matters is that you learn to love people."

In that moment, I looked at my host father and saw him in a completely different light. Here was a man who had once been a stranger to me, but sitting next to me was Dmitry, a tall Russian who had opened his heart and home to me. Because of his generosity and because I had decided to reach beyond my own walls, he was able to become not only my friend but also a father figure in my life.

I thought about my father, who had lived on the other side of the Berlin Wall and had once believed that Russians were "the enemy." Twenty-five years later, his son was living in the home of a former Soviet, eating wafers,[21] talking about politics, and having deep, life-changing conversations.

The literal fall of the Berlin Wall not only signified the end of the Cold War between nations but also opened up the possibility for warm relations between people.

---

21. Some thoughts about Russian wafers: they are delicious, they are delightful, and they are the primary pastries of Heaven. Don't argue with me. I called and asked.

7

The Heart of Russia

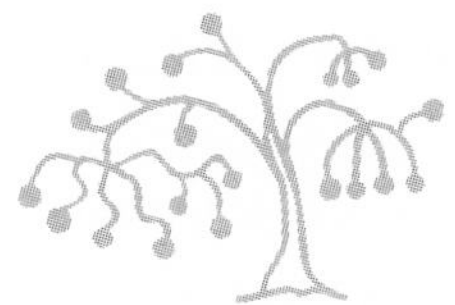

> There are no ordinary people. You have never talked to a mere mortal. Nations, cultures, arts, civilizations—these are mortal, and their life is to ours as the life of a gnat. But it is immortals whom we joke with, work with, marry, snub, and exploit—immortal horrors or everlasting splendors.
>
> —C. S. LEWIS, *THE WEIGHT OF GLORY*

When the heart of the Selfish Giant changed, he saw the children no longer as trespassers but as his garden's most beautiful "flowers." The more we grow to love people, the more we understand that our lives are the most beautiful when they are filled with people.

Not long after my conversation with Dmitry, I went for an evening walk on Red Square, the center of Moscow.

I vividly recall that walk. It has since become one of my favorite memories.

I was meeting up with a friend of mine: Vladimir, a man I had served with on my mission in Nakhodka. To this day, it baffles me how in my zeal to hate my mission I had almost completely forgotten about Vladimir.

Born in Ukraine but raised in Russia, Vladimir was the first Russian to greet me after my plane landed in Vladivostok. Although he knew only a few English words and I knew even less Russian, that didn't stop us from becoming friends. Despite the language barrier, we hit it off surprisingly quickly. It seems that Vladimir and I had the same sense of humor—a dangerous thing, to be sure.

To be perfectly honest, we played a lot of pranks and taught each other a lot of "helpful" words and phrases[22] that would eventually get the other into trouble.

Two years later, we were on the opposite side of Russia and walking on the cobblestones of Moscow, reminiscing about our missions. As we talked, we laughed about how it seemed that he and I had mostly just played chess and eaten wafers. We talked about what we were doing now and the plans we had for the future. The conversation rapidly alternated between English and Russian—neither of us proficient in the other's language but fully able to understand each other nonetheless.

---

22. For example, did you know that the omission of the L sound can transform the Russian word meaning "to pray" into the one meaning "to take a bath"? Turns out, that is a very important distinction if you're asking perfect strangers to pray with you.

After a while (and a couple of minor pranks[23]), we reached Red Square. To say that Red Square is beautiful at night is an understatement. To know that you are walking through hundreds of years of history; to pass the graves of revolutionists, leaders, and martyrs; to stand in awe of the impressive bronze statues of Minin, Pozharsky, and Marshal Georgy Zhukov—these can move the soul into deep reflection.

And the sheer brilliance of Red Square! There is simply nothing to compare to it. To see the GUM department store lit up with thousands of white lights, to look upon a snow-glazed St. Basil's Cathedral, or to walk in the shadow of the Kremlin's great and ancient walls is, for me, beyond description. There are no words to describe just how stunningly beautiful Red Square is at night.

However, on that night, I was less interested in the history of the country and the architecture of its malls and walls, and more interested in the people who had gathered on the square.

I remember looking around at all the different people. They were smiling, laughing, and taking pictures. I'm sure there were Russians, Ukrainians, Armenians, Americans, and numerous other individuals whose nationalities I couldn't identify. But I didn't really register the differences. Once again, Erich's words returned—but this time with a force that penetrated every feeling of my heart: "The only thing that matters is that you learn

---

23. Vladimir attempted to convince a few American girls that it was good luck for foreigners to kiss native Russian men at a "famous" location on the sidewalk. As luck would have it, Vladimir always seemed to be standing at that particular location—no matter where we went.

to love people. If you learn to love the people you are serving, then everything will just fall into place."

For the first time, I started to regret my decision to leave Russia. But this feeling of regret wasn't prompted by shame or guilt—it was prompted by the realization of what I had given up: the opportunity to love and serve people whom I would probably never meet. I never would have met Erich, Galena, or Vladimir had I never gone to Russia. What other people—what other added moments of life—had I denied myself because I decided to build a wall?

Somewhere on those cobblestones of Red Square, I stopped Vladimir and tried to apologize for leaving Russia. I tried to tell him how sorry I was for not being a better friend to him. He looked back at me and furrowed his eyebrows. "No," he said, shaking his head. "You don't need to apologize. You my brother."

Somewhere on those cobblestones, near the red walls of the Kremlin and the colorful towers of St. Basil's Cathedral, my heart melted—winter had officially ended. Like the Giant, I felt the light and could finally see that the most beautiful flowers were the people around me.

Interestingly enough, the name Red Square does not refer to the red bricks of the surrounding buildings; the word *red* in the Russian language has several meanings. In its archaic form, the word красная (*krasnaya*) meant both "red" and "beautiful." During the sixteenth century, the merchants that traded on the square nicknamed it "beautiful" because of the breathtaking presence of St. Basil's Cathedral.

But there's an even deeper meaning to the color red. In American culture, red has been associated with anger, horror, blood, and death—all very negative connotations. But in the Russian culture, the color red is almost the exact opposite. Red is the color of passion, of revolutionary growth, of the blood that keeps us alive, and is a symbolic color for the sun.

Red, therefore, means both light and life. In a poetic sense, as I was standing on Red Square, I was standing on the very heart of Russia.[24] And in the heart of Russia, my heart was changed.

Five years later, almost to the day, I was standing on Temple Square[25] in Salt Lake City, Utah. Despite the chill wind, the sun was rapidly melting the snow, and the brightly colored flowers of spring were pushing through the remaining patches of white.

It was the wedding day of Galena, my dear friend from Nakhodka. Several years into her studies, Galena had fallen in love with Jacob, a kindhearted American man, and they decided to get married. Their ceremony was first spoken in English and then in Russian, and as I sat there listening to it, I thought about how beautifully symbolic that moment was.

Here, at the altar of marriage, the very symbol of sacrifice and love, were two hearts that were dedicating their lives to one another. But their love would not have been possible had physical and metaphorical walls not been torn down. Present at the

---

24. Remember Shannon's heart-shaped keychain?
25. From Red Square to Temple Square, from one experience with a Russian to another—parallels flying all over the place!

ceremony were men and women from several nations, come to celebrate the new life that was symbolically about to begin.

In that moment, the lives of hundreds of people—the family and friends of the bride and groom—had ceased to be about walls and boundaries, and were now about sacrifice and love. Two people had chosen to sacrifice the lives they once knew in favor of a more abundant life together.

About a year later, I held Jake and Galena's newborn daughter in my arms. The tiny baby curled in and quickly fell asleep. "Look at that," said Galena with a smile. "She loves her Дядя Сет."

Fortunately, Galena didn't notice the tears that welled up in my eyes when she called me "Uncle Seth" in Russian. After seven years of friendship, Galena had given voice to a previously unspoken understanding: she had become like a sister to me.

In thinking about my experiences with Vladimir and Galena, I can't help but think about how these tender moments wouldn't have been possible if walls hadn't come down—if they hadn't seen a brother in me.

I'm reminded of a powerful and true story shared by the American historian David McCullough. The story takes place during America's War of Independence, shortly after General George Washington suffered a heavy defeat.

> The next morning a unit from Pennsylvania rode in—militiamen, among whom was a young officer named Charles Willson Peale, the famous painter. He walked among these

> ragged troops of Washington's who had made the escape across from New Jersey and wrote about it in his diary. He said he'd never seen such miserable human beings in all his life—starving, exhausted, filthy. One man in particular he thought was just the most wretched human being he had ever laid eyes on. He described how the man's hair was all matted and how it hung down over his shoulders. The man was naked except for what they called a blanket coat. His feet were wrapped in rags, his face all covered with sores from sickness. Peale was studying him when, all of a sudden, he realized that the man was his own brother. ("The Glorious Cause of America," speech, Brigham Young University, September 27, 2005)

Standing with Vladimir on the cobblestones of Red Square, I felt like I had been reunited with a long-lost brother. But in this situation, I was the one who had been frozen in rags while he had always known we were brothers. And my friendship with Galena had taught me that an indescribable power comes to us when we choose to open a door instead of build a wall. It invites others to tear down their own walls and gives us the opportunity for friendship and unity.

Like the Selfish Giant, I had been blessed with an added measure of life because Vladimir and Galena had taught me how to recognize other people as the most beautiful flowers in the garden of my life. Vladimir once told me, "I believe that God makes us appear different so we can be surprised by joy when we discover that we are actually long-lost family."

8

A Light in the Wilderness

Only when we are brave enough to explore the darkness will we discover the infinite power of our light.

—BRENÉ BROWN, *THE GIFTS OF IMPERFECTION*

I now come to the part in The Selfish Giant that made my dad so emotional. It was the moment when the Giant discovered the element that had transformed the garden of his life: light.

For all my talk about our lives being comparable to a garden, I would miss the mark if I didn't write about the ultimate role that the sun—or light—has in transforming our lives.

In his short story, Oscar Wilde personified light as the little boy who helped the Selfish Giant decide to tear down his wall. One winter morning, many years after he had torn down the wall, the Giant looked out his window and saw "a marvelous sight. In the farthest corner of the garden was a tree quite covered with lovely white blossoms. Its branches were all golden, and silver fruit hung down from them, and underneath it stood the little boy he had loved."

As the Giant ran to greet his little friend, he realized that the boy was much more than he appeared to be. "[A] strange awe fell on him, and he knelt before the little child."

Smiling, the child spoke to the Giant. "You let me play once in your garden, to-day you shall come with me to my garden, which is Paradise."

Ultimately, it was this little boy who had inspired the Giant to change. Like sunlight, it was the influence of the boy that transformed the garden from winter to spring.

Whatever your religious beliefs may be, perhaps we can all agree on the overarching power of light—both physical and spiritual. In its essence, light is whatever encourages us to reach higher. Light can overcome winter, chase away darkness, and help us to see things more clearly. There is no progression without light.

Indeed, light is the foundation of what I think is the greatest story ever told. Chances are, you've probably heard this story a thousand times without realizing it. The echo of this story has rippled through time and has become the backbone of nearly every inspirational story, the standard-bearer of true love, and the model of what we should aspire to become.

One of the earliest echoes of this story was heard in ancient Greece. According to their mythology, there was a Titan—a Greek god—by the name of Prometheus. It is said that Prometheus not only created humans but also saved them.

For secretly, the gods feared that humans had the potential to climb to the top of Mount Olympus—their home—and become their rivals. In order to avoid this, the gods kept men and women to the ground by withholding the one thing that could enable them to become greater—the gift of fire.

Without fire, men and women were unable to pierce the darkness of night, stay warm, create tools, cook their food, or build weapons to fight wild beasts and monsters. During the day, they wandered in the cold, wet mud, and at night they huddled together in caves for want of warmth.

Looking upon the creation of his hands, Prometheus took pity on the humans and resolved to bring them fire—in direct defiance of the gods.

In the dead of night, Prometheus stole a portion of the eternal flame from Mount Olympus and left his heavenly home to bless humankind with this light.

After showing fire to men and women, he taught them how to build it on their own and how to use it to their advantage. Excited by this new power, humans began to build fires and tools of their own.

From the summit of Mount Olympus, the gods watched as the valley below sprang to life with dozens—hundreds—of fires. Prometheus was nowhere to be found.

Enraged by the actions of Prometheus, Zeus condemned him to an eternal punishment. But what was done was done. In a very real way, Prometheus had started a fire that could never be extinguished. And for the rest of time, humankind would honor and revere Prometheus: the giver of life and light.

Years later, Prometheus was rescued from his torment by Hercules. This action was symbolic in many ways. Being rescued by Hercules—half man, half god—represented forgiveness and reconciliation between heaven and earth.

The story of Prometheus teaches us something else about the nature of giving life. Prometheus, a Titan-god, descended the heights of Mount Olympus to give power and aid to humankind—the depressed and downtrodden. Years later, Hercules, a man, while on the upward spiral of becoming a god, rescued Prometheus from a painful punishment. This irony reinforces the truth that in lifting others, we also lift ourselves.

Ultimately, though, the story of Prometheus is but an echo of a greater story. Do you recognize it? It is the story of sacrificing one's own life—one's own needs—to bring light and life to others. It is the story of a painful sacrifice, followed by glorious growth.

This story is so important that it is repeated over and over and over again. Literature is overflowing with characters that sacrifice their lives—literally or figuratively—to bring life to others. The darkened history of our world is made hopeful by the starlight of individuals who have lived their lives as lights for others.

Religions are sustained by the loving sacrifices of men and women who lay down their lives out of love for another. "Greater love hath no man than this," said Jesus, "that a man lay down his life for his friends."

On a more personal level, the story of Prometheus is also an echo of our birth. Our mothers put their own lives at risk to give us life. Through their painful sacrifice, we leave the darkness of the womb and are brought into the light of the world.

Perhaps the reason why this story is repeated so often is that it contains the most important lesson we could ever learn. It teaches us that in order to live a full and abundant life, we must receive light and share it with others.

There is something inside of us—perhaps an ember from that first Promethean fire—that encourages us to defy gravity and reach for the heavens. Indeed, this light comforts us in the midst of death and despair and entreats us to end the cold wars within our hearts. It is this same light that gives us the strength to move forward and step into the greater light of day.

It is this light that gives us the inner strength to tear down our selfish walls, climb our own Mount Olympus, or plunge into the dark to offer light to others.

Not long ago, I was hiking with some friends in Arizona. It had been a long and difficult daylong hike though a narrow, treacherous canyon. Toward the evening, part of our group started to lag behind. Being in the front, I thought nothing of it. After all, we were experienced hikers. We knew what we were doing, and we knew that we needed to set up camp before nightfall. Arizona could be intensely hot during the day, but the temperature often dropped dramatically at night. Coupled with our sweat-soaked clothes, this sudden drop in temperature had the potential to induce hypothermia.

Just as the sun was beginning to set, four of us reached a suitable campsite. The other four were still somewhere in the canyon. We set up shelters, built a fire, and put out some of our clothes to dry. All that took about an hour, but the other four were still missing. We waited impatiently for another half hour.

Still, no one.

We began to think that something bad must've happened and that we needed to go back and help the others. To make matters worse, our portion of the group had only two adults (including me).[26] One of us needed to stay behind with the youth while the other went back into the canyon—alone.

Much to my dismay, the group nominated me to be the solitary figure of the rescue operation. They said it was because I had worked in a wilderness therapy program and therefore had "experience" doing this sort of thing. I also vaguely remember hearing a quiet "You can do it," a half-hearted "It's not that bad," and a somber "You only live once."

I smiled weakly and looked back at the mouth of the dark canyon. It grinned back at me as if to say, "Yeah, so I ate your friends. You wanna die, too?"

As I shakily gathered my things and rummaged through my bag for my headlamp, I tried my best to swallow my fears. But I have to be honest: I didn't want to go into the canyon. I was genuinely afraid of what might happen. Not only was the canyon dark, with boulders and cliffs to worry about, but the night predators were coming out—and I would be alone.

But something happened when I found my headlamp: I remembered the story of Prometheus. Doubtless, he was terrified of leaving the safety of Mount Olympus and taking light to the darkened world below. He knew what it might

26. That is, if you consider me an adult. Use your imagination.

mean for him. But it wasn't about him. It was about the people he loved.

I stared at my headlamp and thought about all the people who had come to find me when I was struggling in the darkness. Their actions were simple, but the effect of those actions had been lifesaving. And now my friends were literally struggling in the darkness. This wasn't about me, it was about them.

So I took a deep breath, switched on my headlamp, and walked into the darkness.

About a half mile down the canyon, I started to hear the voices of my friends. I called to them and they hollered back excitedly. "Seth!" one of them shouted. "I never thought I'd be so glad to hear your voice!"[27]

Using the light from my headlamp as a guide, the four hiked over to me. They were all OK. As it turned out, one of them had eaten something that had made him so sick that they had no choice but to linger behind until the sickness had subsided.

I led them to camp, where they huddled around the warm fire and expressed their gratitude to be out of the canyon. Some of them even thanked me for going back into the canyon to rescue them.

But you know, the more I've thought about that "rescue mission," the more I've realized just how small my role was. Intimidating though it was, all I did was offer a light in the wilderness. That's it. They did all the hard work of moving forward.

---

27. I'm not quite sure what to make of his comment.

Reflecting on that moment has illuminated my understanding about the nature of helping others: small and seemingly simple things can make a big difference. My family and friends shined their small lights to help me out of the wilderness of my darkest struggles: my brother Sean stayed by my side, my sister Shannon gave me a keychain, my friend Jeff wrote me an e-mail, and my mother slept on the floor.

We can't move the noonday sun to light the paths of others, but we can bring our own light to them. We don't need to do big, earth-shattering things to help another move forward, but we can do small things: a kind word, some gentle encouragement, a helping hand, a phone call, or an act of forgiveness and reconciliation.

These things may seem like small gestures, but they are reflections of the life-giving light of the sun, and they will invariably guide wanderers to a greater light.

9

The Resurrected Russian

[T]hou have been benighted till now, wintered and frozen, clouded and eclipsed, damped and benumbed, smothered and stupefied till now, now God yet comes to thee, not as in the dawning of the day, . . . but as the sun at noon, to illustrate all shadows.

—JOHN DONNE, SERMON

"And when the children ran in that afternoon, they found the Giant lying dead under the tree, all covered with white blossoms."

The Giant dies? thought six-year-old me. How awful! What kind of a story is this? But although it seemed morbid to me at the time, Oscar Wilde was using the Giant's death to hint at a much greater life. The fact that the children find his body covered with the white blossoms of spring is symbolic of the life he had given to others.

Not far from Red Square is the statue of a giant among men—a man whom I call "the resurrected Russian." The story of his life began in the nineteenth century, at the height of imperial Russia. During his twenties, he lived in the city of St. Petersburg and was, by the standards of his day, a man of promising talent. To the casual onlooker, this aristocratic and highly educated young man had it all and more to spare.

As if that weren't enough, this young man had an incredible gift with writing. But his favor was about to wear out. For although he was aristocratic and gifted, almost any praise and fame he attained was almost immediately erased by his hotheaded arrogance and contempt for criticism. He was irritable, introverted, stubborn, and cheeky, with a distaste for people and a propensity for drinking and gambling. His foolish arrogance and his utter lack of tact led him to associate with the Petrashevsky Circle, a literary group with socialist leanings and writings that criticized the Russian government.

In April 1849, by order of Czar Nicolas I, the members of the Petrashevsky Circle, and this young writer (their "coconspirator"), were arrested and sentenced to prison. There, they were to await an inevitable execution.

Notice the irony: here was an aristocratic man of talent and education—a man who possessed great potential and promise. Yet despite his tremendous advantages in life, his reckless and selfish lifestyle had forced him to surrender all of it.

He was chained and led into a prison, it is true. But the physical prison was a mere manifestation of his inner prison.

Through his selfishness, this young man had forged the chains of his imprisonment long before he was arrested. For as Nathaniel Hawthorne wrote in *The House of the Seven Gables*, "What other dungeon is so dark as one's own heart! What jailer so inexorable as one's self!"

In December of that same year, this young man and his associates were led to Semyonov Square in St. Petersburg, Russia. After months of imprisonment, they were to be executed by firing squad.

One can only imagine the thoughts and feelings that must have been racing through this young man's mind. Just a month before, he had turned twenty-eight years old behind the bars of a Russian prison. Now his short, once-promising life was about to be extinguished forever.

But at the last moment—indeed, at the very moment when the soldiers raised their guns to fire—an order came to halt the execution. In a miraculous turn of events, the czar pardoned this young man and his associates.

But although their lives had been spared, the czar had commuted their sentence to four years of exile and hard labor in a Siberian prison camp. Classified as a dangerous convict, the young man was shackled and led to a train that would take him to Siberia.

For many Russians, the prospect of life in the frozen wastelands of Siberia was a fate worse than death. As he approached the train, this young aristocrat undoubtedly believed that the summer and sunshine of his life had rotted away into an autumn of decay and a winter of death.

But moments before he boarded the train, the prisoner was approached by a kindhearted woman. Without a word, the woman offered the convict a gift that would forever change his life: a pocket copy of the New Testament.

The young man would carry this book with him for the rest of his life, reading from its pages every day and sometimes reading it out loud to his fellow prisoners.

When he finished serving his sentence, this once hotheaded and selfish young man emerged from prison a changed and humbled man. As he departed Siberia, he carried with him his worn copy of the New Testament. This small gift had not only changed his life but was the foundational inspiration for all of his future novels.

The name of the man was Fyodor Dostoyevsky, and he would become one of the greatest Russian writers of all time, authoring such classics as *The Brothers Karamazov, The Idiot, Notes from the Underground,* and *Crime and Punishment.*

Of all the thoughts and ideas presented in his books, perhaps no theme was more prevalent than the concept of learning to "love thy neighbor." It was a concept that Dostoyevsky's experiences in prison had taught him over and over again.

"The chief thing is to love others like yourself," wrote Dostoyevsky in one of his short stories. "That's the chief thing, and that's everything; nothing else is wanted. . . . And yet it's an old truth which has been told and retold a billion times—but it has not formed part of our lives!" (From "The Dream of a Ridiculous Man")

Once liberated from his Siberian prison, Dostoyevsky spent his life writing about and pursuing this ideal: trying to live one's life for others. He wasn't perfect, and he had his fair share of stumbles, but the measurable difference of his life after Siberia was monumental. Instead of being limited to success in select cities and circles, he became a force of nature in world literature—a powerful, positive force for good.

Today, the body of Dostoyevsky is buried in the city of St. Petersburg. Inscribed on his grave is one of his favorite scriptures: "Verily, verily, I say unto you, Except a corn of wheat fall into the ground and die, it abideth alone: but if it die, it bringeth forth much fruit" (John 12:24).

But the scripture wasn't referring to Dostoyevsky's physical death, for he always believed that his old self had died many years earlier. His pardon and subsequent service in Siberia were the price he paid for a second chance at life: a springtime for the Siberian soul, the resurrected Russian.

The fullness of Dostoyevsky's life after prison is an example and invitation to all to leave the dungeons and wastelands of the heart. To do this, we must be willing to let the old, selfish self "die" and make the change to a fruitful life lived for the benefit of others.

I met a man who "died" once. He was my roommate at college. His name is Ronnie. When I first met him, he told me, "I'm part Tongan, part white, part Chippewa Cree, and part everything else!" He added with a hearty laugh, "Not really sure what I am. At least I'm human, right?"

Whatever he thinks he is, Ronnie is a good man, but he was raised under very difficult circumstances. At a young age, he and his siblings were placed in foster care and were shuffled from home to home. He once told me that wherever he was, he would often call his sister at night so that they could say "I love you" and sing songs to each other.

When he was eight years old, Ronnie and a few of his siblings were adopted by an elderly couple whose own children had grown up and started families of their own. It seemed that things were looking up for Ronnie, but by the time he reached middle school, a bitterness had caught hold of him. His grades dropped, and he became ensnared in drugs and alcohol.

At the age of twenty, Ronnie reached rock bottom. He said that he had come to a point where he didn't care about life anymore. He just wanted to walk in front of a bus and stop feeling forever.

Around the same time, Ronnie found out that he and his girlfriend were going to have a baby. Troubled though he was, Ronnie was excited by the idea of becoming a father. He and his girlfriend began making preparations to start their family.

One day, Ronnie got a call from work. His girlfriend was at the hospital and she needed him to come quickly. Shortly after he arrived, the doctor informed them that their baby had died and that his girlfriend would have to give birth to a stillborn.

Ronnie said that he took it all in stride. He hadn't known the child, so why should it bother him? When the baby emerged, they found out that it was a boy. "He looked just like me," Ronnie told me.

A few hours later, he went back to work. One of his coworkers, a friend of his, heard what had happened and approached Ronnie. He put his hand on Ronnie's shoulder.

"I'm sorry, bro," he said.

Ronnie looked at him and wanted to tell him not to worry—that everything would be fine, but he couldn't. Instead, Ronnie broke down.

The death of his son played a major role in Ronnie's decision to turn his life around. He gave up drugs, alcohol, and cigarettes and aggressively pursued his education. And although he and his girlfriend eventually ended their relationship, they ended it on good terms.

Ronnie once described his turnaround as *"being able to breathe again. It's like coming back to life."* Years later, Ronnie and I worked alongside each other on the ANASAZI trail and helped young people who were going through similar experiences. In a symbolic sense, the old Ronnie had "died" and the new Ronnie was bringing life to others who were struggling. He was helping them to breathe again.

Not long after working on the trail, Ronnie married Noell, a Hawaiian native with a singsong voice and an aura of healing. In December 2012, she gave birth to a son: Jayden Kamauoha Isaacson. According to Noell, Kamauoha (a family name) is Hawaiian for "eternal life" or *"everlasting breath."*

In talking about his experiences, Ronnie said, "Change doesn't happen overnight, but if you set your heart on it and take it step by step, you'll look back and realize you are a better person. Your perspectives will change, and thus your choices—and ultimately your life—will change."

Ronnie's life has always inspired me; it's a testament to the power of change, and it shows how changing our life for good can inspire so much life. In a similar way, if each of us "gave up" our life in the service of others, how much more life would we inspire?

10

The Legend of the Northern Lights

When we love someone, our love becomes demonstrable or real only through our exertion. . . . Love is not effortless. To the contrary, love is effortful.

—M. SCOTT PECK, *THE ROAD LESS TRAVELED*

I wrote the following story not long before my wife and I got engaged. I wrote it in the attempt to crystallize everything I had learned since coming home from Russia. This story, though written by me, doesn't feel like something of my own creation. If anything, it feels like the product of all my experiences with other people. It is a story that has inspired me to follow the light, defy the downward pull of my own selfish nature, and conquer my own mountains.

I share it with you in the hope that it will help you as you try to move forward. It is called "The Legend of the Northern Lights."

It is said that not long after their creation, the salmon lost their way. Aimlessly, they swam in the rivers and waters of Alaska. But in their wanderings, they found neither home nor rest.

Overcome with fear and despair, they began to fight among themselves. But their fighting only deepened their fears and worsened their condition.

Then one day, a legendary being appeared to them at the base of the Great Mountain—a beast of unspeakable wisdom and healing: the White Bear. The Bear came to the edge of the waters and called to the salmon.

"Look to the light of the North Star," said the Bear. "Look to the light and swim to the top of the Great Mountain. There you will find your home. There you will swim in the eternal river of the sky."

The salmon wondered at such a thing. Could it be true? If they followed the North Star, would they be able to swim in an eternal river?

Some of the salmon ignored the White Bear, while others fled in terror. Bears often ate salmon; perhaps his offer was just a clever trap. The smallest of the salmon peeked out of the water and spoke to the Bear. "How can we swim upstream? It is against our nature. We do not have the strength."

"If you look upward and fight onward," replied the Bear, "you can conquer the Great Mountain."

And so it was that those who chose to follow the North Star began the long journey to the summit of the Great Mountain. Swimming upstream was tiring, difficult, and painful. Some of the salmon turned back. Those who remained began to feel discouraged.

"Look to the heavens," reminded one of the salmon.

The other salmon looked up. High above them was the night sky, filled with numberless glittering stars. Despite the darkness of the hour, the light from these stars reminded the salmon of the Bear's promise.

With renewed energy, the salmon fought to swim upstream—growing in strength and desire with every passing moment. As they moved forward, the salmon discovered that they were being filled with a beautiful new light. Their bodies underwent a transformation, changing colors from silvers and grays to magnificent greens and reds.

After a long time of difficult swimming, the salmon made it to the very top of the Great Mountain.

And as they peeked out from the water to look upon the stars, they found—to their astonishment and joy—that they could touch the night sky. It was not an endless expanse of air as they had assumed, but an endless expanse of water.

The night sky was as the White Bear had spoken. It was an eternal river.

These former wanderers wanted more than anything to swim in that water, to live among the stars. But something inside of them held them back. They looked down the mountain to the valley below and distantly saw the other salmon lost in the darkness below. "What about them?" they wondered aloud. "We want to share this joy and happiness with them as well."

As they said these things, the White Bear once again appeared before them. He told them that in order for the salmon to help those who were struggling below, they must swim in the eternal river and become a light for those who were wandering in darkness. But in order to swim in the eternal river, they would have to give up their lives.

Knowing what they truly wanted, the salmon let go of all their doubts and fears, and dove into the night sky—passing from this world into the next. Then, they who had become so full of life and light themselves became the Northern Lights—a river of light to guide the way for others who wander in darkness.

And from their death sprang a new generation of salmon, who swam down the mountainside to show others the way home.

····

EPILOGUE

"So Much Life"

Not long after Kim and I were married, we were on a long drive from Missouri to Illinois. The beautiful countryside prompted a deep conversation about how our lives had led up to our marriage. Somewhere in that conversation, I shared with her the details of my depression and suicide attempt.

Kim and I have been friends since we were fifteen, so she already knew that I had tried to take my life. I had not hidden that from her. But she never quite knew the extent of my struggles, and after I finished telling her everything, I noticed that she had grown very quiet. She stared out the window at the fields and trees passing by. When I asked her what she was thinking, she whispered, "So much life."

"What do you mean?" I asked, furrowing my brow.

"Well, I was just thinking about everything you've done since your recovery and then our relationship and our wedding day. I'm thinking about our memories together and our families. I'm thinking about our travels, the people we'll meet and where we'll eventually end up living. I think about the Christmas cards we'll send to our families and friends, with pictures of us holding our little babies"—at this, Kim started to get emotional. "So much life," she whispered.

Truly, there is "so much life." But that life is found only as we reach above and beyond ourselves. The spring, summer, and abundance of life is achieved only when we tear down the walls and fill our lives with light.

Acknowledgments

As with my story of the Northern Lights, if there's anything praiseworthy in this book (or in my life), it is because of the contributions, the sacrifices, and the light of others. First and foremost, I am profoundly grateful for the love and support of my wife, Kim. Marriage still isn't for me, and you're my heartsong.[28]

But there are others whose light has guided me forward, and my gratitude goes out to them for their patience, love, and beautifully brutal sarcasm[29]:

To my brothers, David and Sean, for teaching me how to laugh. To my sister Jaimie for watching *Friends* with me but also

28. Whatever that means.

29. If you haven't noticed, I greatly appreciate sarcasm.

for being one of my best friends. To my sister Shannon for the letters and keychains, and to my sister Stephanie for the $800 and the things that money can't buy—like having a strong and courageous older sister. To Brett, Kirsten, Ariel, and Josh, for marrying into this sarcastic, standoffish family. To my mother for telling me about the light in the wilderness and to my dad for reading me a story and saving my life.

To Jeff and Juliana, who eagerly jumped at the chance to be the first people to read my manuscript—so they could critique it into oblivion.[30] I'm thankful for their contributions and for their continued friendship.

To Ariel Smith for her humorous and helpful review, to Jason Williams for his brilliant and challenging insight, and to Josh Weed for his creative (and encouraging) contributions. To Ronnie and Noell Isaacson, Galena, Jacob, Vladimir, and Dmitry for allowing me to share their stories.

To the families that have "adopted" me and have shown me what it means to live selflessly.[31] To Brad and Marcy Olsen (and their 7QTPIES)—you gave me far more than Sunday dinners and a place to stay. To the Gonzo family, for the unexpected kinship—it's the leading reason why this Alaskan loves Florida. To the Snyder family—I am convinced that heaven is filled with people like you. To Darryl, whose advice to fill my life with

---

30. Favorite comment from Jeff: "This book needs STRUCTURE!" Favorite comment from Juliana: "No! No! No!"

31. Seriously! They're just like the families in *The Cosby Show* or *Full House*! It's unreal!

light has perpetually guided me forward. And to my in-laws, particularly Hoyt and Margie—not only do they continuously astound me with their faith and courage, but they continuously remind me that I'm their favorite son-in-law.[32] And I like that.

To the people at ANASAZI: Ezekiel Sanchez, Mike Merchant, and Andrew Belcher, and a host of TrailWalkers, RidgeWalkers, YoungWalkers, and one particular Sinagua band in 2010 (Colby Bunderson, Brad Frost, Jake Biggi, Amy Bishop, Brooklyn Lamb, and Matt and Lauren Stanger). There are no words to fully express the things I felt and learned under that Arizona sky, but it all seems to boil down to those precious weeks on Cherry Creek. I've come to the realization that as long as our heart is at peace with others, the dirt roads, narrow canyons, and obstacles of our lives are actually the pathway to paradise. I look forward to seeing you all again at our *final*, "Final D." Keep moving forward.

To everyone at Berrett-Koehler—all of 'em. My association with BK has been one of the greatest blessings of my life.[33] You people are wonderful. Shoot, I'm even starting to like the Editorial Department! To Steve, David, Charlotte, and Anna: thank you for everything. Thank you for taking a risk and believing in me.

But I especially want to single out and thank my editors Jeevan Sivasubramaniam and Neal Maillet. This book would not have happened had it not been for their encouragement

---

32. I'm their *only* son-in-law. I take what I can get.

33. And that's not hyperbole.

and support.[34] Somehow, those two guys managed to become not only my mentors but also my friends.[35] Hope you're ready for some football.

And finally, to Russia—from a quiet harbor in the east to its heart in the west. I do not know what is to come between our two countries, but I do know that I will never rebuild a wall around my own heart. "Come on, [dear friend] (since the strife is past, And friends at first are friends again at last)."[36]

---

34. After I submitted my manuscript, Neal e-mailed me this: "Dude, what is this? You were supposed to write a cookbook?! Nobody will buy this. Back to the drawing board."

35. Like it or not, guys. Don't screw it up.

36. From *A Short History of the Methodists in the United States. to Which Is Prefixed, a Brief Account of Their Rise in England*, by Jesse Lee.

About the Author

Seth Adam Smith is an internationally acclaimed Alaskan-born writer. In 2013, his blog post "Marriage Isn't for You" received over thirty million hits and was translated into over twenty languages. A survivor of a suicide attempt in 2006, Seth has learned that true healing comes from focusing on others and sharing "the Northern Lights of life." He frequently writes about these topics on his website, SethAdamSmith.com.[37]

37. You should check it out. Seriously. I'm waiting.

Berrett-Koehler is an independent publisher dedicated to an ambitious mission: *Creating a World That Works for All.*

We believe that to truly create a better world, action is needed at all levels—individual, organizational, and societal. At the individual level, our publications help people align their lives with their values and with their aspirations for a better world. At the organizational level, our publications promote progressive leadership and management practices, socially responsible approaches to business, and humane and effective organizations. At the societal level, our publications advance social and economic justice, shared prosperity, sustainability, and new solutions to national and global issues.

A major theme of our publications is "Opening Up New Space." Berrett-Koehler titles challenge conventional thinking, introduce new ideas, and foster positive change. Their common quest is changing the underlying beliefs, mindsets, institutions, and structures that keep generating the same cycles of problems, no matter who our leaders are or what improvement programs we adopt.

We strive to practice what we preach—to operate our publishing company in line with the ideas in our books. At the core of our approach is stewardship, which we define as a deep sense of responsibility to administer the company for the benefit of all of our "stakeholder" groups: authors, customers, employees, investors, service providers, and the communities and environment around us.

We are grateful to the thousands of readers, authors, and other friends of the company who consider themselves to be part of the "BK Community." We hope that you, too, will join us in our mission.

A BK Life Book

This book is part of our BK Life series. BK Life books change people's lives. They help individuals improve their lives in ways that are beneficial for the families, organizations, communities, nations, and world in which they live and work. To find out more, visit **www.bk-life.com.**

A community dedicated to creating
a world that works for all

Dear Reader,

Thank you for picking up this book and joining our worldwide community of Berrett-Koehler readers. We share ideas that bring positive change into people's lives, organizations, and society.

To welcome you, we'd like to offer you a free e-book. You can pick from among twelve of our bestselling books by entering the promotional code **BKP92E** here: http://www.bkconnection.com/welcome.

When you claim your free e-book, we'll also send you a copy of our e-newsletter, the *BK Communiqué*. Although you're free to unsubscribe, there are many benefits to sticking around. In every issue of our newsletter you'll find

- A free e-book
- Tips from famous authors
- Discounts on spotlight titles
- Hilarious insider publishing news
- A chance to win a prize for answering a riddle

Best of all, our readers tell us, "Your newsletter is the only one I actually read." So claim your gift today, and please stay in touch!

Sincerely,

Charlotte Ashlock
Steward of the BK Website

Questions? Comments? Contact me at bkcommunity@bkpub.com.